Bedtime Math

THE TRUTH COMES OUT

Bedtime Math®

THE TRUTH COMES OUT

Laura Overdeck

Illustrated by Jim Paillot

Feiwel and Friends
New York

A Feiwel and Friends Book
An imprint of Macmillan Publishing Group, LLC

BEDTIME MATH®: THE TRUTH COMES OUT. Text copyright © 2015 by Laura Overdeck.
Illustrations copyright © 2015 by Jim Paillot. All rights reserved. Printed in the United
States of America by LSC Communications, Crawfordsville, IN. For information,
address Feiwel and Friends, 175 Fifth Avenue, New York, NY 10010.

Feiwel and Friends books may be purchased for business or promotional use.
For information on bulk purchases, please contact the Macmillan Corporate
and Premium Sales Department at (800) 221-7945 x5442 or by e-mail
at specialmarkets@macmillan.com.

Library of Congress Control Number: 2014042416

ISBN: 978-1-250-04775-5 (hardcover) / 978-1-250-07675-5 (ebook)

Book design by Ashley Halsey

Feiwel and Friends logo designed by Filomena Tuosto

First Edition: 2015

10 9 8 7
mackids.com

To Mom and Dad,
for giving me a playful childhood
where numbers were part of the fun.

Introduction

We all know to read to our kids at night, but what about math? Bedtime Math's goal is to make math as common and beloved as the bedtime story: an activity that kids want to do on purpose, the way they seek out playtime or dessert. In this book, we show kids that numbers are fun, and that we're surrounded by math in the most ordinary things around us. Our world becomes that much wackier and more amazing the more we discover the true nature of our regular lives.

It all boils down to making math appealing for kids right from the start. If kids like skateboards, snails, pillow-forts and glitter, then let's give them math about those topics! That's how

I started the Bedtime Math Web site, which serves up a zany new math problem every day. This book and its siblings, *Bedtime Math: A Fun Excuse to Stay Up Late* and *Bedtime Math: This Time It's Personal*, deliver an eye-popping variety of topics with lively color illustrations. In particular, *Bedtime Math: The Truth Comes Out* drives home the magic and ubiquity of numbers with a wild array of surprising facts about our world.

Speaking of facts, these fun math problems give kids the chance to practice *their* math facts. While we don't want to subject our kids to "drill and kill" worksheets and flash cards, kids do deserve the chance to become fast and fluent with numbers. It's not fun to read a book and have to keep stopping to look up vocabulary words, right? In much the same way, it's not fun to learn more challenging topics in math class if you have to keep stopping to re-derive 7 + 4 or 9 x 3. When kids truly understand numbers and can pull up facts in a snap, they can cruise through harder math and enjoy the ride.

And kids aren't the only ones. The fact is, all *grown-ups* need to handle numbers daily, whether or not they're in scientific or technical jobs. Just plain old everyday life requires a sense of numbers. When your teenagers go shopping, they should be able to tell which size pack of paper, pens or snacks is the better buy thanks to the lower cost per item. Years later when your grown children take out loans, they should know how to estimate the long-term overall cost. When voting on a school budget, donating to a charity, or buying a raffle ticket, people need to know how to do quick, back-of-the-envelope math to make good decisions. The alternative is sad and scary: In a recent study, adults who performed poorly on a brief, over-the-phone math quiz did, in fact, have worse credit scores and more precarious finances.* Math-fluent folks live more effective lives and spare themselves a lot of stress.

Beyond daily life, we want to dream as big for our kids as they dream for themselves. Some kids will go on to become inventors and help our society by developing new medicines, clean energy, and radiation-free electronic devices. To fulfill these dreams, they will surely need math, science and technological training.

To give our kids access to a happy future, we want them to love math so they embrace it and dive in whole hog to learn it. And to stoke that enthusiasm, we need serious change in the culture around math in our country. We all know plenty of grown-ups, as well as kids, who don't like math, who find it tedious and even outright nerve-wracking. That outcome is both unnecessary and preventable, and Bedtime Math aims to help.

Each and every day, we're bombarded with more and more information through the Internet, which serves up a mix of accuracy, quasi-accuracy and sheer nonsense. It takes a keen eye to process all of that information, look at it critically and take action. We want to equip our kids to navigate this big and ever-more-complex world around us, to thrive rather than just survive. And Bedtime Math is a fun, cozy place to start the journey.

*Meier, Stephan, et al. "Numerical Ability Predicts Mortgage Default," *Proceedings of the National Academy of Science*, June 24, 2013.

How to Do Bedtime Math—The Fun Way

Don't sweat it. Choose the level of challenge that works best. There's a reason we don't list a "correct" age range for each problem. The three levels of challenge are labeled "Wee ones," "Little kids," and "Big kids" precisely to avoid specific ages or grade levels. The first level is named "Wee ones" to emphasize that kids should start doing math as preschoolers. The more math at home before kindergarten, the better. With **"Wee ones,"** your child can have fun comparing numbers, finding shapes, and counting objects. **"Little kids"** moves your child on to single-digit adding and subtracting, as well as simple logic puzzles. **"Big kids"** introduces the excitement of wrestling with bigger numbers, as they build on all their little-number learning and discover, for instance, that multiplication is just a speedy way to add. And finally, there is the **"Bonus"** level, where readers tackle math acrobatics that require two or more separate steps. All levels, however, are great mental warm-ups for *anyone*, all the way up to the grandparents who use the Web site as a daily brainteaser. So just jump right in, and see what level seems like a comfortable starting point.

It's an activity, not a test. The goal is to have an entertaining conversation that leads to the answer, not to see if your kids can get the answer right off the bat. Read the math problem aloud, then walk through the steps to solve it, and please feel free to give hints when needed. For more pointers, you can also check out the Equation Chart at the back of the book—a.k.a. the math behind the fun.

Don't worry about your kids getting wound up. We haven't seen that happen with Bedtime Math. After all, the time-honored way to fall asleep is to count sheep! Numbers are soothing and predictable, and math problems give kids a reason to settle down and focus. Besides, what better way to end the day than by accomplishing something?

Don't sweat it. Part II. Yes, we'd love to become part of your routine every single day. But we all have those days that begin with the roof falling through to the first floor, and we just can't quite get to every wholesome activity. *Bedtime Math*—this book, as well as all the content on the Web site—is here for you when you're ready for it.

Any time of day can work.

We do talk about nighttime a lot, but Bedtime Math can become a part of any routine: breakfast, carpool, dinnertime, bath time. If you weave it into a daily activity, it can become a natural habit.

Stretch.

Because it's a team effort, you can reach as high as you and your child want to try. There's something magical about adding two big numbers for the first time ever, or multiplying 5 times 5. While teachers can't have that playful one-on-one with twenty-three students at once, you *can* do this at home, and you'll find that kids love to tackle the tougher challenge levels.

It's beautiful.

Again, we never hear people say, "Ewww, a book at bedtime?!" Likewise, there's absolutely no reason to say that about math. Numbers are beautiful, and kids love attention. *Bedtime Math* just puts the two together. With that, let the games begin!

How tall is the bottom half of the Great Pyramid?

Which falls faster, a flying piano or a bowling ball?

What did astronauts do on the Moon?

Can a snake lose its tongue?

Do onions, potatoes and apples actually taste the same?

Have we always had left and right shoes?

Is it good or bad to be bird-brained?

Is there really an Oniontown?

Are bananas really a fruit?

Have carrots always been orange?

Are you really "all in the same boat"?

What words just don't rhyme with anything?

When did Frisbees start flying?

How many ways can you make change for a dollar?

Do astronauts really eat astronaut ice cream?

Are marshmallows actually good for you?

How did chocolate chips end up in cookies?

How hard is it to "hold your horses"?

Who came up with the Popsicle?

Did Christopher Columbus ever really find America?

Can you ever have nighttime all day?

Does a snow globe really shake snow?

What do barns have to do with crayons?

Did Play-Doh start off as a toy?

Ice Cream for All—Even Astronauts

In outer space you can't eat wet, messy food—
the drips and drops will float all over. But you
shouldn't have to miss out on ice cream. So in
the 1960s the Whirlpool Company cooked up
astronaut ice cream. They freeze-dried coconut
fat, sugar, milk fat, and other ingredients
into a bar of non-cold, non-wet ice cream, in stripes
flavored chocolate, vanilla, and strawberry. Did astronauts
ever eat this stuff in space? Yes, once and only once on a trip in 1968,
because it just wasn't that tasty. By 1972 astronauts were eating
regular ice cream in space, and only Earthlings visiting
science museums still eat the dry kind.

Do astronauts really eat astronaut ice cream?

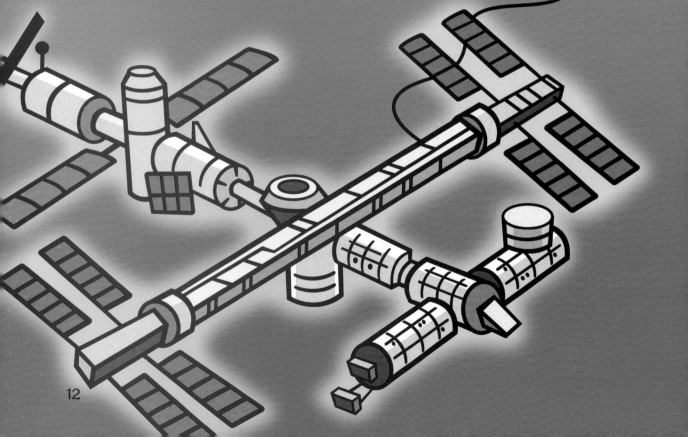

🚀 **Wee ones:** If you're counting up your astronaut ice cream ingredients—coconut fat, sugar, milk fat, and chocolate—what numbers do you say?

🚀🚀 **Little kids:** If you chow down 3 packs of chocolate-vanilla-strawberry astronaut ice cream, how many stripes did you eat in total?

🚀🚀🚀 **Big kids:** If an astronaut unwraps 6 ounces *each* of Moon Mint, Planet Peanut Butter, and Starry Swirl, but 4 ounces crumble and start floating around, how much is left?

⭐ **Bonus:** If your rocket launches at 11:58 a.m. and by 1:11 p.m. you just *have* to eat some astronaut ice cream, how long did you wait?

Eat Your Way Through Town

Is there really an Oniontown?

Chances are your town has a simple town-like name, such as Westfield or Middletown. Town names like that don't say anything very exciting, and we don't wonder what will happen to us when we go there. But there are many towns in America named after foods. You have to wonder how people chose these names: Does Oniontown, Pennsylvania have more onions than any other town? Does Cheesequake, New Jersey have more cheese? We don't even want to ask if Ham Lake, Minnesota has a lake full of ham. At least in Picnic, Florida you can pick whatever food you want, as long as it fits in the basket.

Wee ones: For breakfast you can choose to visit Bacon, Indiana; Buttermilk, Kansas; Hot Coffee, Mississippi; Ham Lake, Minnesota; or Oatmeal, Texas—they're all real towns! How many towns is that, and which one would you visit?

Little kids: If it's only 10:00 a.m. in Sandwich, Massachusetts and they always eat their sandwiches at noon, how much longer do they have to wait to eat?

Big kids: For dessert you can drive 1,100 miles from Chocolate Bayou, Texas to Pie Town, New Mexico, then another 800 miles to Sugar City, Idaho. How far do you drive in total?

Bonus: If half the 300 people in Two Egg, Florida eat 2 eggs each while half eat 4 apiece, how many do they eat in total?

entering PieTowN

Red as a . . . Barn

What do barns have to do with crayons?

Crayola may be the biggest crayon company, but they didn't start off thinking about kids or art or toys. Back in the 1800s, a chemical company called Binney and Smith made red powder so that people could paint their barns red instead of letting the wood turn boring gray. They also made black dye for car tires, which turned out to make them stronger than white tires! After inventing dustless chalk and visiting schools to sell it, they noticed wax crayons could be made better, too. So they started making crayons and changed their name to Crayola. They've moved far beyond red and black, making crayons in mac 'n cheese, mango tango, and more than 120 other colors.

Wee ones: If you draw yellow, red, and orange all together to make your own mac 'n cheese shade, how many crayons did you use?

Little kids: If your box of crayons has red, red-orange, orange-red, violet-red and 3 other colors using red, how many reddish shades do you have?

Big kids: If your giant glow-in-the-dark jungle uses up 5 neon yellow crayons, twice as many neon green, and 3 more blues than yellow and green together, how many crayons do you use up?

★ **Bonus:** The 72-crayon box set includes the cool metallic ones: gold, silver, and copper. What fraction of the whole set is metallic?

Marshmallows for the Soul

Are marshmallows actually good for you?

When we dump lots of marshmallows into our hot chocolate, we're sneaky because we know the marshmallows aren't any better for us than the drink. But those yummy white poofs were once a type of medicine. Long ago, people ate the flowers of the "marsh mallow" plant as a health food. Then in the 1800s the French would grind up the plant's roots, mix that with something gummy to hold it together, and whip it with sugar to make it taste good. We make marshmallows almost the same way today, except we leave out the healthy-plant part . . . and that probably tastes better.

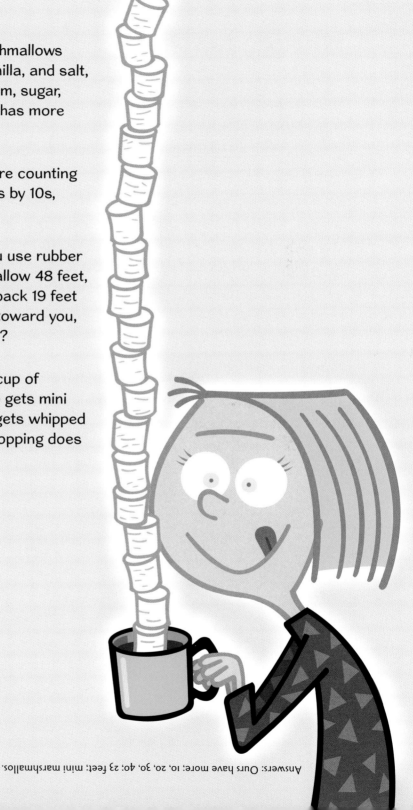

Wee ones: If our marshmallows have gelatin, sugar, butter, vanilla, and salt, and the long-ago ones had gum, sugar, and plant root, which version has more ingredients?

Little kids: If you're counting out a bag of 40 marshmallows by 10s, what numbers do you say?

Big kids: If you use rubber bands to slingshot a marshmallow 48 feet, then it hits the wall, bounces back 19 feet and then rolls another 6 feet toward you, how far from you does it stop?

Bonus: If you make a cup of plain cocoa, then the next cup gets mini marshmallows, then the next gets whipped cream and you repeat, what topping does the 134th cup get?

Whoaaaaah!

How hard is it to "hold your horses"?

Unless you live on a farm, chances are you don't have live horses wandering around your house. So what the heck do people mean when they tell you to "hold your horses"? Luckily, it doesn't mean you have to grab the reins of a bunch of horses and hang on to stop them from running down the street. It just means "Wait a second!" or "Be patient!" and comes from the days before cars, when all our wagons were pulled by horses. The question is, if you *did* have to hold down 6 or 8 horses, would you be strong enough to do it?

Wee ones: Horses each have 4 feet, while people have 2. Who has more?

Little kids: If your friend has to hold 6 horses while you're stuck holding 8, how many more do you have?

Big kids: If you're calmly riding your bike at 14 miles per hour, but your horse starts pulling you twice as fast as that, how fast are you now going?

Bonus: If at the rodeo there are twice as many people as horses and there are 24 feet in total, how many horses are there?

What They Really Did on the Moon

Astronauts have lots of adventures beyond eating space ice cream. In 1969 Neil Armstrong landed on the Moon and planted an American flag on it, which then fell over when the lunar module took off. Other flags planted since then have all been bleached white, because there's hardly any air on the Moon to weaken the sun's light. On the Apollo 14 mission, Alan Shepard hit a golf ball, which flew 6 times as far as it would on Earth thanks to the Moon's weak gravity. And during Apollo 15, David Scott dropped a feather and a hammer, which fell at the same speed since there was hardly any air to help the feather float. It would be fun to go to the Moon and play these games—too bad we all need air to breathe.

What did astronauts do on the Moon?

Wee ones: If astronauts have planted 6 American flags on the Moon, and you fly there and plant 1 more, now how many flags are there?

Little kids: If on Earth you can jump 2 feet up into the air, and on the Moon you can jump 3 times as high, could you moon-jump over a 5-foot flag?

Big kids: If objects stay in the air 6 times as long on the Moon as on Earth, how long would your fancy 4-second high dive somersault take on the Moon?

★ Bonus: Armstrong said they had taken "one small step for man," but that step was probably 4 feet long! If we normally step 16 inches, how many times as long was their "small" step on the Moon?

Going Bananas

Are bananas really a fruit?

When we think about fruit, we almost always picture apples, oranges and bananas. But bananas are a weird fruit compared to the others. No really, they're pretty weird: the banana plant is an herb, just like basil or oregano, and that yellow stick we call a banana is the berry of that plant. And unlike a grape or a strawberry, you can't plant this fruit to make a new banana plant; you have to cut off part of another banana plant and put that new branch in the ground. Luckily banana plants grow very easily and spread like crazy—hence the saying "going bananas."

Wee ones: If your pet monkey has 2 bananas and you have 2 apples, how many fruits do you have together?

Little kids: A banana tree can grow 20 feet in height in just one year. If *you* could grow even half that amount in a year, how tall would you be a year from now?

Big kids: If you sneak 3 banana plants into the town playground and the plants triple in number each year, how many plants will the playground have 2 years from now?

Bonus: How many ways can a hungry gorilla divide 36 bananas into smaller equal-size bunches (2 or more in each)?

Answers: 4 fruits; different for everyone (add 10 feet to your height); 27 plants; 7 ways: groups of 2, 3, 4, 6, 9, 12, and 18.

Weight a Minute . . .

Do you have what it takes to lug sand?

When you stand on the beach and let sand fall from your hands into the breeze, it all blows away into the air, often into some unhappy person's face (maybe even your own). What's hard to believe is that fluffy sand is really, really heavy. If you've ever tried to lug a pail of it from the water to your sand castle, you've probably wondered how that powdery stuff can weigh so much. Well, it turns out that a 1-foot cube of wet sand weighs a whopping 100 pounds! Even 1 cubic foot of dry sand weighs 50 pounds, and a little shoe box of it weighs 20 or 30 pounds. Building that giant sand castle is actually a giant workout.

 **Wee ones:** Which is heavier, 5 pounds of water or 5 pounds of sand?

Little kids: If your sandcastle pyramid stacks 1 cup of sand on top of 2 cups on top of another 3 cups, how many cups is that?

Big kids: If a 2,300-pound rhinoceros is charging toward you, and you can block him with a wall of sand that weighs the same, how many 100-pound buckets of sand do you need?

⭐ **Bonus:** If that 2,300-pound rhino is joined by his 2,800-pound cousin, now how many 100-pound buckets of sand match their weight?

Who Chopped Down That Cherry Tree?

George Washington, the first president of the United States, was obviously a pretty awesome guy all around. But is it true that he always told the truth? And did he really chop down a cherry tree? Sort of. According to a long-ago book by Parson Weems, a friend of the Washington family, George was given his own little ax as a 6-year-old. He excitedly tried it out on a cherry tree and scraped off a lot of bark, which made it die. When questioned by his dad, George 'fessed up. Now, if only we knew whether Abe Lincoln really walked 17 miles to the library . . .

Is it true that George couldn't tell a lie?

🍒 **Wee ones:** If George had really chopped down a tree each day for a week, how many trees would he have chopped?

🍒🍒 **Little kids:** If George counts that he's chopped down 14 trees, then goes wild and chops down 4 more, what numbers would he say to count those new ones?

🍒🍒🍒 **Big kids:** If a tree's 20 branches could each be cut and sanded into 4 boards, how many boards would George have scored to build a cool canoe?

⭐ **Bonus:** If each tree branch could make 1 toy boat *or* 3 books for President Lincoln, how many of each could George have made from 10 branches to make twice as many books as boats?

You Say Potato, I Say White Onion . . .

Do onions, potatoes and apples actually taste the same?

Onions are one of the smelliest foods out there, thanks to the sulphur they give off. And "smelliest" doesn't usually mean "tastiest." That said, if you plug your nose and bite into an onion, suddenly it won't taste like much at all. In fact, if you hold your nose and take a bite of an onion, an apple and a raw potato, they won't taste that different from each other! Try it and see! But be careful, because those onions will still make your eyes water.

Wee ones: How many tears is the onion-eating boy shedding?

Little kids: If you plug your nose and taste an onion, then an apple, then a potato, and repeat over and over, what's the 7th bite that you take?

Big kids: If on a dare you can chew an onion for 23 seconds before your eyes water, and your friend can last 17 seconds, how much longer did you last?

Bonus: If you eat 13 ounces of each of these 3 semi-smelly foods, how many ounces do you eat in total?

Close, but No Cigar

Did Christopher Columbus ever really find America?

We always talk about how Christopher Columbus discovered America, right? Well, it's time to set the record straight. First of all, Columbus never made it to America's mainland. In 1492 he landed on the island now called the Bahamas, which he thought was part of Asia. Even after 3 more round trips from Spain, he *still* never reached America, nor realized that these islands were not Asia. America is named after Amerigo Vespucci, the Italian explorer who landed in Brazil in 1499. Amerigo was the one who figured out that this was a "New World," and that's why America isn't called Christophica.

Wee ones: What shapes are the sails on Columbus's ship here?

Little kids: If Columbus sailed west to the Bahamas on the 1st leg of his trip, then east back to Europe on the 2nd, then back to the Bahamas on the 3rd . . . which way was he sailing on the 7th leg?

Big kids: How many years after Columbus's 1492 trip did Amerigo reach the New World for real?

★ Bonus: When did America celebrate the 500th anniversary of Columbus's 1492 voyage?

BRAZIL

Can you ever have nighttime all day?

Where It's Never Bedtime

As the Earth zooms around the Sun, it also spins, but at a tilt. So part of the year the northern half of Earth tilts toward the Sun and gets hot—which is "summer," from June to September—and the southern half gets its hot summer during the opposite time of year, from December to March. What's crazy is that in summer, the farther north you go, the *longer* the sun stays up during the day . . . and once you cross the Arctic Circle, the sun stays up around the clock! Then in winter it's the opposite: it stays dark all 24 hours, while the penguins in the sunny south have no bedtime at all.

Wee ones: If Antarctica is sunny just 3 hours today and just 2 hours next Tuesday, which day gets more sun?

Little kids: If your penguin friend has had 21 days with no nighttime, how many nonstop sunny days in a row will it be tomorrow?

Big kids: If the penguins finally fall asleep and nap 3 hours today, 4 tomorrow and 5 the next day, how much sleep do they get?

Bonus: If you like your 9 hours of sleep, but the sun goes down only from 11:30 p.m. to 2:15 a.m., how much time do you need to sleep in broad daylight?

Stick in the Mud(sicle)

Who came up with the Popsicle?

Way back in 1905, an 11-year-old kid named Frank Epperson was stirring a bucket of powdered soda and water to make soda, also called "pop." He left the stick in the bucket overnight by accident, and the whole thing froze. The next morning he pulled out the stick, and found a giant, bucket-shaped chunk of fruit-flavored ice on the end of it. That's how the "pop"-sicle was invented. We make our Popsicles a lot smaller these days, though—there's no need to eat a dessert the same size as your whole head.

Wee ones: Are you older or younger than Frank was when he made the first Popsicle?

Little kids: If you put toothpicks in ice cube trays filled with mango-papaya punch, you can make mini-Popsicles. If you make 43 and give them away in sets of 10, how many extras are left for you?

Big kids: How many mini-Popsicles can you make using 3 12-cube trays?

⭐ **Bonus:** If a box of Popsicles has 4 lemon and 4 orange Popsicles, what are your chances of picking 2 of the same flavor?

Answers: Different for everyone—compare your age to it; 3 mini-Popsicles left; 36 mini-pops; 3/7 (since you have 3 choices left of the same flavor, but 4 of the other flavor).

Pyramid Scheme

The Great Pyramid is a huge, triangle-sided building in the hot deserts of Egypt. It's about 5,000 years old, and took more than 20 years to build. It would have been weird to watch that pyramid grow over time. The bottom of the pyramid is really wide, while the pointy top doesn't use that many stones. So just the bottom 1/5 of the pyramid uses up half the stones! It probably took up half the total time to build, too. In fact, by the time you climb halfway up the pyramid, you've passed 9/10 of the stones. So it didn't take as many guys to stack those last few stones on top—and hopefully none of them were afraid of heights.

Wee ones: If a pyramid has 4 triangular sides and a bottom square one, how many "faces" is that?

Little kids: If you build a flat Lego triangle with 4 bricks on the bottom, 3 bricks on the row above and 2 at the top, how many bricks did you stack?

Big kids: About 9/10 of the Great Pyramid's stones are in the bottom half. What fraction of stones is in the top half?

Bonus: If the bottom 1,800,000 stones are 9/10 of the total, how many stones are in the top half?

On the Wrong Foot

Have we always had left and right shoes?

It doesn't feel good when you put your shoe on the wrong foot. It squishes your big toe and the top of your foot. But for thousands of years shoes didn't have a left and a right: A pair of shoes were exactly the same. Only about 200 years ago did shoemakers start making a different left shoe and right shoe. Let's face it, it had to be easier to sell shoes when people didn't have to match a right with a left. But our feet are probably happier now.

Wee ones: How many shoes are in 1 pair?

Little kids: If you wear a shoe on each foot, a shoe on each hand, and a shoe on your head, how many shoes are you wearing?

Big kids: If you have 26 properly matched leopard-print boots, how many *left* boots do you have?

⭐ **Bonus:** If a store has 12 purple right shoes and 9 purple left shoes, and you grab any 2 shoes without looking, what's the *greatest* number of un-pairable shoes that could remain?

Answers: 2 shoes; 5 shoes; 13 boots; 5 right shoes (if you grab 2 left shoes).

Off the Wall—Forever

Did Play-Doh start off as a toy?

Play-Doh is so colorful and squishy. You can roll it into balls, flatten it into pancakes, cut it into stars or squeeze it into spaghetti strands. But Play-Doh began life as the least exciting thing ever: wallpaper cleaner. Back in the 1930s, wallpaper was made of real paper and got very dirty, so people would slap "Kutol" (CUT-all) onto it to peel off the dirt. When vinyl wallpaper came along, people stopped buying those cans of Kutol, and the company almost went out of business. But one teacher figured out you could *play* with Kutol by smushing it into shapes, and the rest is sticky history.

⭐ **Wee ones:** If you have 6 cans of Kutol and use 1 as Play-Doh, how many cans are left?

⭐⭐ **Little kids:** If you take your cans of Kutol and dye one orange, then one lime green, then one electric blue, then one hot pink, then one orange to start over, what colors do you dye the next 3 cans? See if you can remember!

⭐⭐⭐ **Big kids:** If a can of blue Play-Doh can make either 4 blue giraffes or 16 blue frogs, how many animals can you make if you use ½ the can for giraffes and ½ for frogs?

⭐ **Bonus:** If you make a *giant* giraffe as tall as a house, and you need 128 cans of blue Play-Doh for the body plus ⅛ as many orange cans for the spots, how many cans do you need?

Chips on the Loose

How did chocolate chips end up in cookies?

The chocolate chip cookie must have taken a lot of work to invent. How else could we end up with such a perfect mix of vanilla and chocolate and crunchiness and gooeyness? Well, the whole thing was actually an accident. In 1930, Ruth Wakefield tried to make chocolate cookies by throwing pieces of solid chocolate into the batter, thinking the chocolate would mix in as it melted. But it didn't mix: The chocolate melted but the chips stayed whole, giving us the polka-dot dessert we call the chocolate chip cookie. If only all mistakes worked out this well.

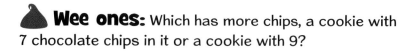 **Wee ones:** Which has more chips, a cookie with 7 chocolate chips in it or a cookie with 9?

Little kids: If you pick up a gooey 5-chip cookie and 3 melted chips drip into your lap, how many chips are left in your hand?

Big kids: A 1-cup measure equals 16 tablespoons, and a tablespoon holds roughly 10 chips . . . about how many chips fit in 1 cup? And can you eat them all in one sitting?

⭐ **Bonus:** If you bake 36 cookies and ½ are peanut-butter chip while another ⅓ are mint chip, how many are regular chocolate chip?

Answers: The 9-chipper has more; 2 chips are left; 160 chips; 6 cookies.

45

That Sinking Feeling

Are you really "all in the same boat"?

When someone tells you "We're all in the same boat," it doesn't mean you're all actually floating around in a boat on a lake. It means you're all facing some big bad problem, and it's going to get worse for all of you together. In a real boat, the more people in that boat, the more likely it's going to sink. A boat can carry the same weight as the weight of the water it "displaces," or pushes out of the way as it sinks—at least until the water washes over the top. If your boat has low walls, you're in trouble.

🚢 **Wee ones:** Which one is longer, a 6-foot canoe or an 8-foot sailboat?

🚢🚢 **Little kids:** If you and 45 friends all get sopping wet running through the sprinkler, how many of you are "all in the same boat?"

🚢🚢🚢 **Big kids:** If 17 kids say the dog ate their homework and twice as many say their pet snake ate it, how many kids are all in the same boat?

⭐ **Bonus:** If a boat can hold at most 5,000 pounds of stuff, and right now you can load only 101 more pounds, how much weight is the boat already carrying?

Rhyme Time

What words just don't rhyme with anything?

You can walk the talk, and fix a mix of sticks, and eat a sweet beet. But you can't flurple a purple, even if you want to. They say there are no English words that rhyme with month, orange, silver and purple. One smart guy did figure out that a "chilver" is a female lamb, and that "curple" is another way to say "crupple," the back end of a horse. For the other two, you can make up your own words to rhyme . . . but when you tell someone to pat your pet bilver or sit on a skorange, no one will have a clue what you're talking about.

Wee ones: How many letters does "month" have?

Little kids: If you change purple to skurple, how many more letters does your new word have?

Big kids: If your 8 pet wilvers each eat 7 durples a day, how many daily durples do you serve?

⭐ **Bonus:** If you own 6 silver bilvers and 9 times as many silver wilvers, how many total silver things do you have?

SKORANGE

SMORANGE

BLORANGE

Answers: 5 letters; 1 more letter; 56 durples;
60 silver things (6 bilvers, 54 wilvers).

Bird-Brained

Is it good or bad to be bird-brained?

When we say someone is bird-brained, usually we don't mean anything good by that, as most birds don't seem too smart. An ostrich's brain is even smaller than its eyeballs (which are almost as big as tennis balls). So ostriches get confused when they're being chased, and end up running in circles. On the other hand, a lot of birds' brains are big compared to their body weight, and some birds do act smart.

Scientists have shown that crows understand numbers, that parrots can count to 6, and that some birds can use objects as tools. We humans had better start studying to keep up.

Wee ones: If your parrot Polly can count to 6, what numbers does she know how to say?

Little kids: If 13 Egyptian vultures are cracking eggs open with rocks, while 2 crows poke insects out of a log using sticks, how many tool-using birds do you have?

Big kids: If you know 20,000 words and your parrot knows 1/10 as many, how big is your parrot's vocabulary?

Bonus: Ostriches are super-speedy but not super-smart runners. If your ostrich runs 130 feet but runs ½ of that in circles before catching on, how far did the ostrich run in circles?

As Purple as a Carrot

Have carrots always been orange?

We love carrots for their crunchiness and fun orange color. But carrots weren't always orange. They used to be red, yellow, purple, and white. Then in the 1500s the Dutch joined red and yellow carrot plants while growing them in order to make orange carrots, since Holland's royal family was called the House of Orange. Since carrots still grow in all those colors, if we just added blue and green we could have a whole rainbow of carrots.

52

Wee ones: If you have those 4 crazy carrot colors plus orange, how many carrot colors do you have?

Little kids: If you have 1 red carrot and 1 purple one, how many white carrots do you need to make a stack of 10?

Big kids: If you have 5 pieces of magenta broccoli, 18 fluorescent red string beans and 6 periwinkle potatoes, how many wrong-colored food items do you have?

★ **Bonus:** If the Dutch had taken red, yellow, purple and white carrots and combined each color with one of the other 3, how many different carrot colors could they have invented?

Bugging Out

Are ladybugs really ladies?

Okay, let's get a few things straight. A firefly can fly, but isn't made of fire. A butterfly can fly, too, but isn't made of butter. A praying mantis preys (catches animals for food), but doesn't pray. Ladybugs aren't all ladies, and daddy long legs aren't all daddies, or even boys at all—and they also aren't spiders! But a walking stick really looks like a stick that can walk, and unfortunately, stink bugs really do stink—so stay away from those.

Wee ones: Which has more spots, an 8-spotted ladybug or a 10-spotted ladybug?

Little kids: How many legs is the mantis waving if he's standing on 4 of them? Remember, all insects have 6 legs.

Big kids: How many legs do a firefly, a butterfly, a ladybug, and a praying mantis have all together? Again, all insects have 6 legs. . . .

Bonus: If 28 cheerleader ladybugs stand in a pyramid with 1 in the top row, 2 in the next, etc., how many would stand in the bottom row holding everyone up?

Putting the Pea in Peanut

Is a peanut a pea or a nut?

A house in a tree is a treehouse, and a cake in a cup is a cupcake. Then what the heck is a peanut? It turns out peanuts are more like peas than nuts: they're part of the pea family. Ever notice how they come 2 at a time inside a shell, just like peas in a pod? Also, while most nuts grow on trees, peanuts grow from the ground on a vine, just like peas. That may be why you can be allergic to peanuts but not to other nuts. Meanwhile, almonds are actually related to the peach family—just to make things really nutty.

🥜 **Wee ones:** If you eat 6 peas and 7 nuts, of which food do you have more?

🥜🥜 **Little kids:** If you grab 5 peanut shells and there are 2 nuts in each, how many peanuts do you have?

🥜🥜🥜 **Big kids:** If you shoot the peas from 8 5-pea peapods through a straw, how many peas go flying?

⭐ **Bonus:** If the first peapod you pick has 4 peas, the next has 6 peas, the one after has 9, and the one after that has 13, how many are in the 5th peapod? Continue the pattern.

Answers: Nuts: 10 nuts; 40 peas: 18 peas (Add 5 to follow the pattern, having already added 2, then 3, then 4).

The Tall Keep Getting Taller

Mount Everest is the tallest mountain in the world. At 29,035 feet tall, it edges out even other giants like Kilimanjaro in Africa. But for some reason that isn't enough for old Everest. Mount Everest

Who's growing faster, you or Mount Everest?

is growing ¼ inch per year! That's because the big, rocky slabs of earth under it are mashing together and pushing the mountain upward. You, as a kid, are growing faster than the mountain—maybe a couple of inches a year—but you aren't made of rock, so it's easier for you to stretch.

Wee ones: How many mountain climbers can you count here?

Little kids: If Mount Everest grows ¼ of an inch a year, how long does it take to grow 1 inch?

Big kids: Mount Everest was first measured at 29,002 feet in 1841. How much taller is it now at 29,035?

Bonus: When you turn 32 years old, how much will Mount Everest have grown during your life?

29,035 feet

And growing!

Worth a Fortune

Who really invented the fortune cookie?

Fortune cookies are those crunchy squares of dough wrapped around a slip of paper that somehow predicts what's going to happen to you, even though anyone else could have opened that cookie. Lots of Chinese restaurants serve them at the end of the meal, but fortune cookies aren't from China, and weren't even invented by anyone Chinese! Historians think they were first made in Japan, and showed up in the United States in the early 1900s. Also, the fortune cookies back then were shaped like a tube, not a triangle. Were those fortunes truer than the ones you pick today?

expect the unexpected

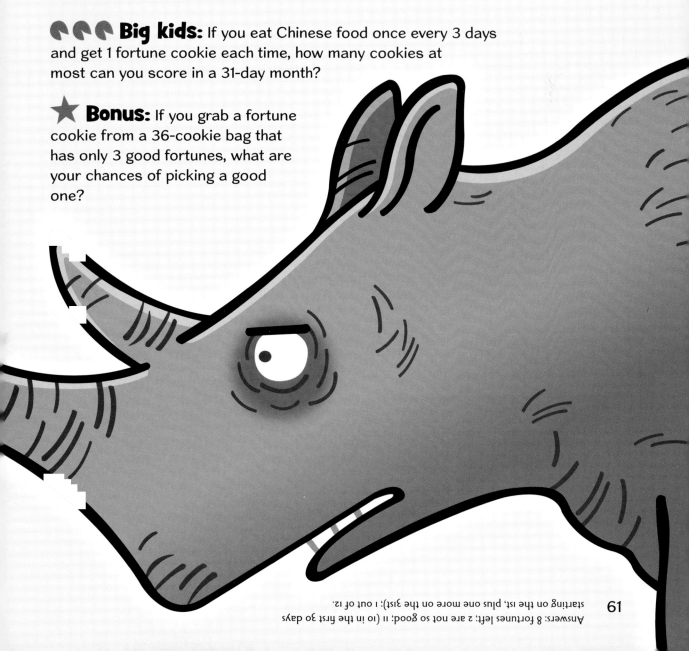

Wee ones: If you grab 9 fortune cookies and snap 1 open, how many fortunes do you have left to read?

Little kids: The fortune inside the cookie can be good or bad. If you have 7 fortune cookies and 5 are good, how many aren't so good?

Big kids: If you eat Chinese food once every 3 days and get 1 fortune cookie each time, how many cookies at most can you score in a 31-day month?

Bonus: If you grab a fortune cookie from a 36-cookie bag that has only 3 good fortunes, what are your chances of picking a good one?

Answers: 8 fortunes left; 2 are not so good; 11 (10 in the first 30 days starting on the 1st, plus one more on the 31st); 1 out of 12.

A Real Scare

How do scarecrows scare those scary crows?

Scarecrows, those funny stick figures wearing plaid shirts stuffed with hay, don't stand around in the field just to decorate the place. Farmers build scarecrows to scare away, well, crows, since crows eat crops. But scarecrows scare the birds not by looking like people, but by *smelling* like people. By wearing our clothes, scarecrows smell like us, and birds apparently don't think we smell good. Is it the ketchup we spilled on ourselves, or the apple juice? Either way, birds know to stay away.

Wee ones: If that scarecrow has 2 crows sitting on its arms and 1 on its head, how many crows is it not scaring away?

Little kids: Who has more fingers, you or that scarecrow?

Big kids: If you have 5 smelly shirts and 4 smelly pairs of pants for your scarecrow, how many different smelly outfits can you make for him?

Bonus: If a crow can smell you from 7 feet, how many *inches* is that?

Answers: 3 crows; you do; 20 outfits (4 for each of the 5 shirts); 84 inches.

Great Bubbly Mistake

Is soda good for you?

Soda is always the bad guy: the sugary drink that will rot your teeth and make you fat. But soda *used* to be good for us. Starting in the late 1700s, drug stores made medicine taste better by mixing it with water, some bubbles, and flavoring. Soon these drinks tasted so yummy that people drank them even while totally healthy, and soda—or pop—was born. Since then, soda has become less and less good for you . . . today's soda has tons of sugar and dyes, so don't think you can guzzle it down to get healthy.

🥤 **Wee ones:** If you mix a bucket of pop on Tuesday, then let it freeze through the next day and pop it out the day after that, what day do you get to eat your giant Popsicle?

🥤🥤 **Little kids:** If you're mixing a cherry-pineapple soda that needs 10 drops total of flavoring, and you've mixed in 7 drops of cherry, how many drops of pineapple flavor do you need?

🥤🥤🥤 **Big kids:** Chewable vitamins are tasty *and* good for you. If a jar has 12 orange vitamins, half as many cherry vitamins, and 6 more grape than cherry, how many vitamins are in there?

⭐ **Bonus:** If you eat 257 vitamins this year and twice as many next year, how many *more* do you eat next year?

Shake Them Bones

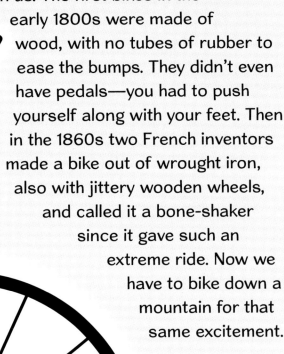

What's a bone-shaker, and does it really shake your bones?

When you ride a bike, those big, bouncy tires give you a nice smooth ride. But bicycles weren't always so easy on us. The first bikes in the early 1800s were made of wood, with no tubes of rubber to ease the bumps. They didn't even have pedals—you had to push yourself along with your feet. Then in the 1860s two French inventors made a bike out of wrought iron, also with jittery wooden wheels, and called it a bone-shaker since it gave such an extreme ride. Now we have to bike down a mountain for that same excitement.

✸ **Wee ones:** How many bicycle wheels can you count on the right-hand page here?

✸ ✸ **Little kids:** If you grab 4 bicycles and a 1-wheeler, called a unicycle, how many bone-shaking wheels do they have all together?

✸ ✸ ✸ **Big kids:** If you ride a bone-shaker and 7 of your 22 teeth fall out, how many teeth do you have left?

★ **Bonus:** If you get a flat tire 1/4 of the way into your 48-mile ride, how far do you have left to walk?

Staring Contest

Which animal has the longest, strongest stare?

We don't think much about eyelids, but eyelids
are our friends. They keep our eyes wet and push
away dust and dirt. Some animals, like fish and snakes,
don't have eyelids at all. That's fine for fish—their eyes stay watery all
the time—but how do snakes sleep with no eyelids? (They sleep with
their eyes open—their brains can still switch off to sleep.) Meanwhile,
camels totally lucked out: each eye has *three* eyelids, one of which is
clear so the camel can see through it during desert sandstorms.
But in a staring contest, the snakes and fish will win.

Wee ones: Who has more eyelids, you or a camel?

  Little kids: If a camel has 3 lids on each eye, how many lids does it have all together?

   Big kids: If you can hold a 13-minute stare without looking away and your pet snake lasts twice as long, how long can your snake hold the stare?

⭐ **Bonus:** Who blinks more lids, 15 camels or 24 people?

A Meal Fit for an Earl

Did sandwiches ever have sand in them?

A sand sandwich doesn't sound very tasty.
Thankfully, people don't make that for lunch. A
sandwich holds not sand, but thin slices of meat, cheese,
lettuce or other goodies between those two pieces of bread.
It's named after the Earl of Sandwich, who liked playing card games
so much that he wanted to hold and eat his sloppy dinner at the
same time. The bread as the food-holder fixed that problem, and the
sandwich was born.

Wee ones: If you can eat a sandwich, play cards, and play a piano with your toes at the same time, how many activities are you doing at once?

Little kids: If you stack 13 layers in your sandwich and 3 of them are fried green tomato, how many layers use some other food?

Big kids: If you invent the super-tall "Ate a Gator" Sandwich, with a repeating pattern of bread, a slice of alligator steak, cheese, lettuce, then bread again, gator and so on, what number layer is the 3rd slice of cheese?

Bonus: If you layer bread, gator, cheese, lettuce, then back to bread to repeat, what's the 30th layer?

THIS EXIT
Food
Gas
Time Alone

51

ente

Give Me a Sign

Who's bigger, you or that stop sign?

When you drive, you see all kinds of colorful signs:
road signs to tell you where you are, and traffic signs
like STOP and DO NOT ENTER. Since you're speeding by while
trying to read them, those signs have to be big—*way* bigger than
you think. Those cute red stop-sign octagons are actually 2 ½ feet
tall! Never mind the green highway signs: they're 12 feet from top to
bottom, and that little blue and red shield with the interstate number is
3 feet tall. Those signs look small from far away, but if you stood next
to one, you'd look a *lot* smaller.

Wee ones: If you're just 1 foot taller than the 3-foot rectangle of a speed limit sign, how tall are you?

Little kids: The letters saying EAST or WEST on interstate highway signs are 12 inches tall—a whole foot—and the city names are 4 inches taller. How tall are the city letters? Try counting up!

Big kids: If you're 4 feet tall, and the green rectangular interstate sign has a 3-foot shield symbol, 3 rows of 2-foot letters and 3 feet of blank space, how much taller than you is that sign?

Bonus: If you can reach 52 inches high and your dog can reach 28 inches, can the two of you stack to reach a stop sign 7 feet off the ground?

Answers: 4 feet tall; 16 inches; 8 feet taller (sign is 12 feet); not quite! (you'll reach 80 out of 84 inches)

73

Money That Grows

Does money grow on trees?

You might hear a grown-up say, "Money doesn't grow on trees, you know." That just means money isn't easy to get. And it's true, money does not grow on trees. However, American paper money *does* have all kinds of plant stuff in it. Not only is every dollar bill made of wood, like any paper, but the wood pulp also has cotton and silk mixed in to make the paper stronger. So can we grow money? Better yet, if it's made of cloth, can we wear it?

74

$ **Wee ones:** Which is worth more, a $5 bill or a $10 bill?

$ $ **Little kids:** If you make a paper hat out of 4 $1 bills and a $5 bill, how much is that hat worth?

$ $ $ **Big kids:** You can fold 8 bills into an origami Frisbee. If they're all $5 bills, how much is that Frisbee worth?

★ **Bonus:** What if you pitch a mini tent made of 200 $20 bills— how much is that tent worth?

Answers: The $10 bill; $9; $40; $4,000!

Time Flies

Which insect thinks time runs fastest?

They say "time flies when you're having fun," because that's when each minute feels too short. Of course, a minute is a tiny slice of your life: if you live 76 years, that's about 40 million minutes! But for insects, time must feel different. Fruit flies and worker bees live for only 4 to 6 weeks, so an hour for them feels like a month for us. It's even worse for mayflies: after growing in a sac for 2 years, they pop out and live for less than 24 hours. That said, at least all these guys get to fly.

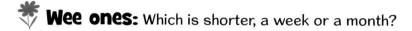

🌼 **Wee ones:** Which is shorter, a week or a month?

🌼🌼 **Little kids:** Snails have it easy: they can sleep for 3 years straight. If you start a 3-year nap when you're 6, how old are you when you wake up?

🌼🌼🌼 **Big kids:** If a worker bee lives only 6 weeks, how many days is that?

⭐ **Bonus:** If a fruit fly lives just 1 week, how many *hours* is that?

Waffling on It

We eat our food off dishes, but sometimes we get to eat the dish itself. The ice cream cone came to life at the World's Fair in 1904 when an ice cream seller ran out of bowls, so a pastry chef passing by wrapped a waffle into a cone shape to hold the ice cream. It was a huge hit. Meanwhile, an Italian man named Italo Marchiony also invented the ice cream cone that same year; it was just that good of an idea. Today our ice cream cones are crunchy, but they still have those square designs to remind us how they began.

Why do ice cream cones have squares on them?

Wee ones: What shape does a cone look like from the side?

Little kids: If your ice cream cone will melt in 10 minutes and you've been eating it for 3, how much time do you have left?

Big kids: If a waffle cone can hold 1 huge scoop of ice cream, how many waffles do you need to hold 14 scoops of Cauliflower Crunch and 17 scoops of Shark Tooth Swirl?

Bonus: If you have a waffle cone with 6 rows of 6 squares and you've munched through 1/3 of those squares, how many squares are left to eat?

When You're as Slow as Plants

What strange things happen to the sloth?

The sloth might be the slowest, laziest mammal out there. It sleeps 20 hours a day, and moves only when it has to; even then its top speed on the ground is 6 to 7 feet per minute. Having extra toes doesn't seem to help, either: the 3-toed sloth is just as slow as the 2-toed sloth. In fact, sloths move so little and so slowly that plants grow on them! Algae, which is green, seaweed-like muck, grows right on their fur, turning the sloth green. This helps sloths blend safely into the trees, which is handy when they're settling in for an 18-hour nap.

Wee ones: Who has more toes, the 2-toed sloth or the 3-toed sloth?

Little kids: Sloths all have 4 feet with the same number of toes on each. So how many more toes does the 3-toed sloth have than the 2-toed one?

Big kids: If a sloth sleeps 19 hours in one day, how many hours did it bother to stay awake?

Bonus: If you, your friends and some 2-toed sloths have 104 toes in total, and there are twice as many sloths as people, how many sloths are there?

Answers: The 3-toed: 4 more toes (12 vs. 8); 5 hours; 8 sloths (since each set of 2 sloths and a person has 26 toes total, and 4 of those sets cover 104 toes).

Tongue in Cheek

Can you imagine having all your skin peel off and land on the floor still in the shape of a person? That would be mighty weird, but snakes do this 2 to 4 times every year. Snakes "shed" because as they grow, at some point the skin can't stretch enough to fit anymore. The snake rubs against trees and rocks to help shed the skin, which comes off in one whole sock-like piece, including the tongue. By the way, we people shed skin, too, but just in teeny bits at a time . . . a lot less alarming.

Can a snake lose its tongue?

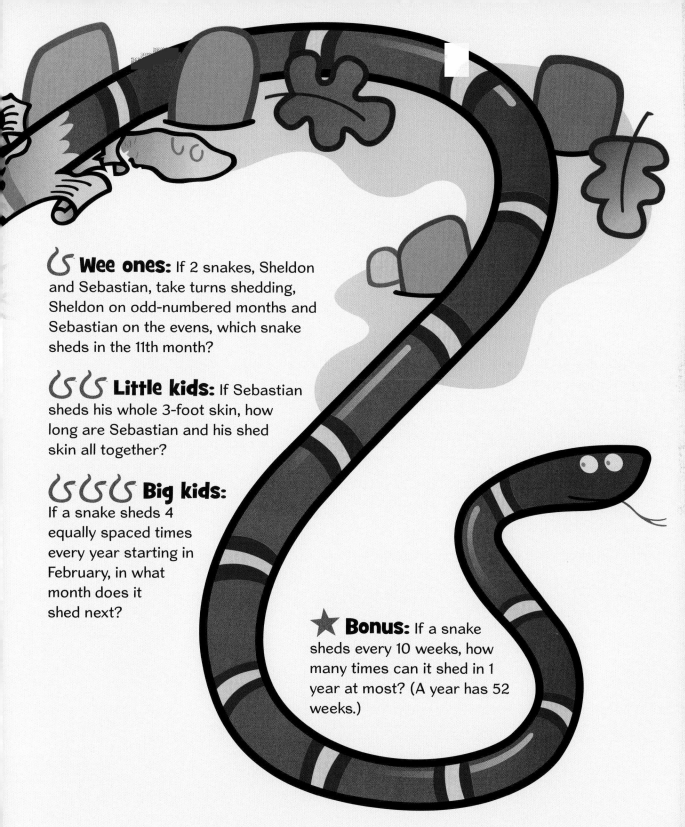

Wee ones: If 2 snakes, Sheldon and Sebastian, take turns shedding, Sheldon on odd-numbered months and Sebastian on the evens, which snake sheds in the 11th month?

Little kids: If Sebastian sheds his whole 3-foot skin, how long are Sebastian and his shed skin all together?

Big kids: If a snake sheds 4 equally spaced times every year starting in February, in what month does it shed next?

⭐ **Bonus:** If a snake sheds every 10 weeks, how many times can it shed in 1 year at most? (A year has 52 weeks.)

Let It Snow

Does a snow globe really shake snow?

Snow globes are those balls of clear plastic or glass filled with water, fun tiny objects like buildings or toys, and white sparkles. When you shake a snow globe, the white flecks swirl to make a mini snowstorm. So what are those snowflakes, anyway? They're called "flitter," and they used to be chips of bone or porcelain, or even sawdust. The longer they float and the more they shine, the better. Now many are made of plastic. The good news is, whatever the flitter is made of, it won't melt in any weather.

Wee ones: Pretend to shake your snow globe and try to count all the flakes. Try counting as high as you can!

Little kids: If you shake your Statue of Liberty snow globe for 2 seconds and the flitter takes 9 seconds to sink, how long did that whole snowstorm take?

Big kids: If a snow globe contains 3 teaspoons of "snow" with 200 flecks in each teaspoon, how many flitter flakes does the globe have?

Bonus: If your snow globe plays a 3-minute song and your flitter sinks just 20 seconds into it, how much song is left?

Over the Edge

If you throw a marble, a bowling ball and a piano off the roof at once, they'll all hit the ground at the same time. That's because an object that weighs twice as much needs twice as much force to move it, but gravity works twice as hard on that bigger object, so it evens out. The man who figured out why was Isaac Newton, who's famous for having an apple land on his head and getting the idea. That probably isn't exactly what happened—he probably just watched an apple fall— but thanks to him, we know if we jump off the roof carrying a piano, it won't turn out well for us.

Wee ones: If you *did* roll a marble, a bowling ball and a piano off the roof, how many things would go hurtling into the air?

Little ones: If it takes 8 seconds for a beach ball to bounce down the stairs but ½ as long if you just toss it over the railing, how fast does it fall to the ground?

Big kids: If you toss your stuffed animal up into the air and clap 5 times before catching it, then 8 times on the 2nd toss, then 14 times on the 3rd toss, then 23 times on the 4th, how many speed-claps do you clap on the next toss? Continue the pattern.

Bonus: If 1 bowling ball weighs the same as 100 marbles, and the piano weighs the same as 100 bowling balls, how many marbles match the weight of a piano?

Which falls faster, a flying piano or a bowling ball?

Answers: 3 flying things; 4 seconds; 35 claps (You add 12 to follow the pattern, since you've added 3, 6, and 9); 10,000 marbles.

Pie in the Sky

When did Frisbees start flying?

Frisbees are those flat plastic circles that you can throw with all your might and send sailing through the air. We don't know who exactly threw the very first one, but we do know that the first bunch of Frisbees were actually pie plates. In the 1800s the Frisbie Baking Company sold their pies in lightweight tins. College students soon discovered that once they'd eaten the pie out of them, the tins flew really well. In 1948 the first plastic Frisbee, spelled with two e's, was invented by Walter Morrison (whose dad, by the way, invented the first sealed-beam car headlight). So now we can throw our plates without sending pie crumbs flying.

Wee ones: If you throw 5 cream pies and 1 gushes out of the plate in midair, how many pies stay in?

Little kids: If you toss 15 Frisbie strawberry-rhubarb pies and your friend catches 10 of them, how many Frisbie pies splat on the ground?

Big kids: If you can eat 3 chocolate caramel cream pies a day, how many days till you have 27 empty tins to throw?

★ **Bonus:** If kids started throwing Frisbie tins 80 years before the first Frisbee, when did they start throwing them?

Time for a Change

How many ways can you make change for a dollar?

When you buy something worth less than a dollar using a $1 bill, the store owes you money back. The money they give back to you is called "change," and we use coins when this is a small amount: a penny for 1 cent, a nickel for 5 cents, a dime for 10 cents, and a quarter for 25 cents. With just those 4 types of coins, you can make an incredible number of combinations: there are 242 ways to make a full dollar of change, and if you mix in half dollars, too (50 cents), there are 292 ways! Luckily, the guy at the store needs to figure out only one way.

¢ **Wee ones:** How many pennies can you count on this page?

¢¢ **Little kids:** How many dimes does the store need to give you to make 20 cents of change?

¢¢¢ **Big kids:** If you have one apiece of the 5 coins—a penny, a nickel, a dime, a quarter and a half-dollar—how much are they worth together?

★ **Bonus:** How many ways can you use dimes, nickels or both to buy some 50-cent blinking glow-in-the-dark shoelaces?

Answers: 10 pennies; 2 dimes; 91 cents; 6 combinations (10N, 8N+1D, 6N+2D, 4N+3D, 2N+4D, 5D).

91

EQUATION CHART
THE MATH BEHIND THE FUN

Title	Wee ones	Little kids	Big kids	Bonus
Ice Cream for All—Even Astronauts	1,2,3,4	3+3+3=9	(6x3)-4=14	1:11 p.m.-11:58 a.m. =1hr 13min
Eat Your Way Through Town	Count 5 towns	12:00-10:00=2 hrs	1,100+800= 1,900	(300/2)x2+ (300/2)x4=900
Red as a . . . Barn	Count 3 colors	4+3=7	5+(2x5)+3+ (5+[2x5])=33	3/72=1/24
Marshmallows for the Soul	Count 5 ingredients vs. 3	10,20,30,40	48-19-6=23	134-(44x3)=2
Whoaaaaah!	4>2	8-6=2	14+14 or 14x2=28	24/[4+(2x2)]=3
What They Really Did on the Moon	6+1=7	(3x2)>5	6x4=24	(12x4)/16=3
Going Bananas	2+2=4	height+(20/2)	3x3x3=27	Divisors of 36
Weight a Minute . . .	5=5	1+2+3=6	2,300/100=23	(2300+2800) /100=51
Who Chopped Down That Cherry Tree?	1+1+1+1+1+1=7	Count up from 15 to 18	20x4=80	3(10-t) books= 2t books
You Say Potato, I Say White Onion . . .	Count tears in picture	Onion-apple-potato to 7th item	23-17=6	13x3=39
Close, but No Cigar	Triangles and rectangle	7 is odd	1,499-1,492=7	1,492+500=1,992
Where It's Never Bedtime	3>2	Next number after 21	3+4+5=12	9-(2:15 a.m.-11:30 p.m.)=6hr 15min
Stick in the Mud(sicle)	Your age > or < 11	43-4 sets of 10	12+12+12 or 12x3=36	(3 of same flavor) /(7 left in total)
Pyramid Scheme	4+1=5	4+3+2=9	1-9/10=1/10	1,800,000/9 is 1/10th of total
On the Wrong Foot	A pair is 2	2+2+1=5	26/2=13	12-(9-2)=5
Off the Wall—Forever	6-1=5	o-g-b-p, then o again	4/2+16/2=10	128+128/8=144

Title	Wee ones	Little kids	Big kids	Bonus
Chips on the Loose	7<9	5-3=2	16x10=160	36-36/2-36/3=6
That Sinking Feeling	8>6	45+1=46	17+(2x17)=51	5,000-101=4,899
Rhyme Time	Count 5 letters	7-6=1	7x8=56	6+(6x9)=60
Bird-Brained	Count to 6	13+2=15	20,000/10=2,000	130/2=65
As Purple as a Carrot	4+1=5	10-(1+1)=8	5+18+6=29	RY, RP, RW, YP, YW, PW
Bugging Out	10>8	6-4=2	6x4=24	1+2+3+…+7=28
Putting the Pea in Peanut	7>6	2+2+2+2+2, or 2x5=10	8x5=40	4+2, then +3, +4, +5
The Tall Keep Getting Taller	Count climbers	4x1/4=1	29,035-29,002=33	32/4=8
Worth a Fortune	9-1=8	7-5=2	# of 3s in 31 starting on 1	3/36=1/12
A Real Scare	2+1=3	10>8	5x4=20	7x12=84
Great Bubbly Mistake	Tuesday, Wednesday, Thursday	10-7=3	12+12/2+(12/2+6)=30	257 is 1/2 of 257+257
Shake Them Bones	Count wheels	2+2+2+2+1=9	22-7=15	48-48/4=36
Staring Contest	6>2	3+3=6	13+13 or 13x2=26	15x6>24x2
A Meal Fit for an Earl	1+1+1=3	13-3=10	Bread-gator-cheese-lettuce to 3rd cycle	30-(7x4)=2
Give Me a Sign	3+1=4	12+4=16	3+(3x2)+3-4=8	76x12>52+28
Money That Grows	10>5	1+1+1+1+5=9	8x5=40	200x20=4,000
Time Flies	Week<month	6+3=9	7x6=42	7x24=168
Waffling on It	Triangle	10-3=7	14+17=31	6x6-(6x6/3)=24
When You're as Slow as Plants	3>2	4x(3-2)=4	24-19=5	2x[104/(2x8+10)]=8

Title	Wee ones	Little kids	Big kids	Bonus
Tongue in Cheek	Odds vs. evens	3+3=6	May is 12/4 months after Feb	1+ 10s up to 51
Let It Snow	Count as high as possible	2+9=11	3x200=600	(3x60)-20=160
Over the Edge	Count flying items	8/2=4	5+3, then +6, +9, +12	100x100=10,000
Pie in the Sky	5-4=1	15-10=5	27/3=9	1,948-80=1,868
Time for a Change	Count pennies	10x2=20	1+5+10+25+50 =91	10N, 8N+1D, 6N+2D, 4N+3D, 2N+4D, 5D

© Kathryn Huang

Laura Bilodeau Overdeck is the author of *Bedtime Math: A Fun Excuse to Stay Up Late*, *Bedtime Math: This Time It's Personal* and *Bedtime Math: The Truth Comes Out*. When she and her husband, John, started giving their three children zany math problems at bedtime, friends asked if she'd share these riddles, and Bedtime Math was born. It has since grown into a nationwide movement to make math cool and to get kids fired up about numbers, sparking Bedtime Math's new afterschool math club, Crazy 8s. Laura holds a BA in astrophysics from Princeton University and an MBA from the Wharton School of Business.

bedtimemath.org

Thank you for reading this Feiwel and Friends book.
The Friends who made

Bedtime Math®

THE TRUTH COMES OUT

possible are:

Jean Feiwel
publisher

Liz Szabla
editor in chief

Rich Deas
senior creative director

Holly West
associate editor

Dave Barrett
executive managing editor

Lauren A. Burniac
editor

Nicole Liebowitz Moulaison
production manager

Anna Roberto
associate editor

Christine Barcellona
administrative assistant

Follow us on Facebook or visit us online at mackids.com.

OUR BOOKS ARE FRIENDS FOR LIFE